My birthday

What's your name?

1 **Read. Then complete.**

1

Sally

What's her _name_ ?

2

Tommy

_____ his name?

3

Debbie

Fred

_____ name _____
Debbie.

_____ name _____
Fred.

1 Is it purple?

2 Unscramble. Then write.

1
name Tim . My is

My name is Tim.

2
red ? it Is

_____

3
it What ? is colour

_____

4
are old ? you How

_____

3 Read. Then match.

1 What colour

2 Is it

3 No, it

4 It

a isn't.

b is green.

c purple?

d is it?

4 **Read. Then write and colour the cakes.**

1

I'm eight. <u>My</u> favourite colour _____ pink.

2

I'm ten. My _____ colour _____ yellow.

3

I'm three. _____
_____
_____ purple.

5 **Write for you. Then draw and colour.**

I'm _____
_____
_____
_____ .

2 At school

What's this?

1 **Read and match. Then draw and colour.**

What's this?

		1
brown	backpack	

a	purple	pencil case	2

It's

	yellow	chair	3

an			

	orange	book	4

② Read and circle. Then draw and colour.

1 What are (*this* / *these*)?
   They (*is* / *are*) blue pencils.

2 What (*is* / *are*) this?
   It (*is* / *are*) a brown desk.

3 What are (*this* / *these*)?
   (*It* / *They*) are red pens.

4 What (*is* / *are*) this?
   It (*is* / *are*) a ruler.
   What colour (*is* / *are*) it?
   It (*is* / *are*) green.

3 **Find the questions. Use the code. Then look and answer.**

	▲	★	■	●
1	see	drums	many	How
2	see	can	can	fish
3	How	you	you	many

▲ 3   ■ 1   ● 2   ★ 2   ■ 3   ▲ 1

1 <u>How</u> _____ _____ _____ _____ _____ ?

● 1   ● 3   ★ 1   ■ 2   ★ 3   ▲ 2

2 _____ _____ _____ _____ _____ _____ ?

My family

This is my brother

1 **Unscramble. Then write.**

1

(brother)   (is)   (This)   (my)

This _____ .

2

(ten)   (He)   (is)

_____ .

3

(is)   (This)   (sister)   (my)

_____ .

4

(is)   (seven)   (She)

_____ .

2 Look and read. Then circle.

	artist	doctor	cook	farmer	vet
Mum	✗	✗	✗	✗	✔
Dad	✗	✔	✗	✗	✗
Granny	✔	✗	✔	✗	✗
Grandad	✗	✗	✗	✔	✗

1 Is Mum a vet?   Yes, she is. / No, she isn't.

2 Is Grandad a cook?   Yes he is. / No, he isn't.

3 Is Dad a doctor?   Yes, he is. / No, he isn't.

4 Is Granny a farmer?   Yes, she is. / No, she isn't.

3 Draw a person in your family. Then write.

This is my _____ .

Is _____ an artist?

_____ .

What does she want to be?

4 **Look and write. Use the words from the box.**

a	wants	What	cook	she	does	to	doctor	He

1

What _____ Jane want to be?
She wants to be a _____ .

2

This is Sue. What does _____
want to be?
She _____ to be a _____ .

3

Bill's favourite colour is blue.
_____ does he want to be?
He wants _____ be an artist.

4

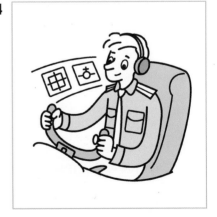

This is my brother, William.
_____ wants to be _____
pilot.

4 My body

I've got two arms

1 Read and match. Then write.

1  2 3

a

I've got three legs.
I've got two heads.
I've got eight eyes.

b

I've got one head.
I've got two eyes.
I've got three legs.

c

_____

_____

_____

_____

2 Read. Look at Activity 1. Then write (✔) or (✗).

1 I'm monster 2.
I've got two heads, eight eyes and three legs.

2 I'm monster 1.
I've got four eyes, three arms and four toes.

3 I'm monster 3.
I've got nine fingers, four legs and two wings.

3 **Unscramble and write. Then draw.**

green　　He's　　heads　　two　　got

1 _____

got　　fingers　　eight　　blue　　He's

2 _____

three　　three　　He's　　feet　　got　　legs　　and

3 _____

4 She's got ...

④ Look and write. Then draw. Use the table.

I've	got (a)	green	jumper
She's		yellow	trousers
He's		purple	dress
		red	skirt
		black	shoes
		pink	socks
			hat

1 I've got green trousers and a yellow hat.

2 She's _____

_____

3 He's _____

_____

My pets 5

What's that / are those?

1 **Look and read. Then circle.**

1 What are (*that* / *those*)? (*It's* / *They're*) frogs.

2 What (*is* / *are*) that? (*It's* / *They're*) a rabbit.

3 What are (*that* / *those*)? (*It's* / *They're*) mice.

2 **Write the question. Then draw.**

1 What's _____ ?

It's a parrot.

2 _____ ?

They're snakes.

Read. Find the question and answer.

Have ➡ you				haven't	.		
	got		No	I	I've	got	.
	a	cat	?			two	parrots

Have you _____

_____ ?

_____

_____

_____ .

Unscramble. Then answer.

you rabbit Have a ? got tall

1 Have you got a tall rabbit?

✔ Yes, _____ .

got small ? you Have tortoise a

2 _____

✘ _____ .

Has three he hamsters ? got young

3 _____

✔ _____ .

she snake got Has long a ?

4 _____

✘ _____ .

⑤ Look. Then write (✔) or (✗).

	🐍		
🐱	🐶	🐹	🐱
🐶	🐶	🐢	🐱
Martha	Tom	James and Liz	Sue

1 Tom has got two dogs and a snake. ✔

2 Martha hasn't got a tortoise. She's got a hamster. ☐

3 James and Liz have got three pets. ☐

4 Sue's got two kittens. ☐

⑥ Look at Activity 5. Then answer.

1 Has Martha got a kitten? _Yes_ , _She_____ .

2 Has James got a hamster and a dog? _____ , _____ .

3 Has Tom got two dogs? _____ , _____ .

4 Has Sue got a puppy? _____ , _____ .

6 My house

Where's ...?

1 Look. Then write (✔) or (✗).

1 My brother is in his bedroom. ✔

2 My sister is in the garden. ☐

3 Granny and Grandad are in the living room. ☐

4 Mum and Dad are in the bathroom. ☐

2 Look at the answers. Then write the questions.

1 <u>Where are his mum and dad?</u>   In the garden.

2 _____   In the bathroom.

3 _____   In the living room.

4 _____   In the bedroom.

3 Read. Then draw.

There's a sofa in the living room.

There's a cooker in the kitchen.

There are two lamps in the bedroom.

There's a shower in the bathroom.

There are two kittens in the living room.

4 Match.

a

b

1 living room   **2** bedroom   **3** bathroom   **4** kitchen

c

d

6 Where do you live?

5 Follow. Then write.

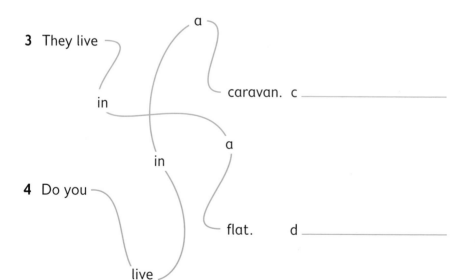

1 Where do
a
house.   a _____

you

2 Do you live

in   live?   b *Where do you live?*

3 They live
a
caravan. c _____
in
a
in
4 Do you
flat.   d _____
live

Food 7

I like / don't like ...

1 **Read and write (✔) or (✘). Then write.**

1 chicken	✔	I _like_ chicken.
2 yoghurt	☐	I _____ yoghurt.
3 fruit	☐	I _____ fruit.
4 milk	☐	I _____ milk.
5 cheese	☐	I _____ cheese.
6 salad	☐	I _____ salad.
7 bread	☐	I _____ bread.
8 lemonade	☐	I _____ lemonade.

2 **Look at the table. Then write questions and answers.**

	fruit	salad	meat
Mike	✔	✘	✔
Tracy	✘	✔	✔

Mike

1 What do you _want_ ? _____ want fruit.

2 _____ do you like? I _____ fruit and meat.

I _____ like salad.

Tracy

3 What do _____ want? I _____ salad.

4 What do you _____? I like salad and _____.

I don't _____ fruit.

7 Do you like ... ?

3 **Complete the questions. Then circle your answers.**

1

Do you like vegetables?

Yes, I do. / No, I don't.

2

_____ like jelly?

Yes, I do. / No, I don't.

3

_____ like cake?

Yes, I do. / No, I don't.

4 **Unscramble. Then answer.**

honey	Do	like	?	you

1 _____

_____ .

?	like	Do	you	lemonade

2 _____

_____ .

chocolate	Do	?	you	like

3 _____

_____ .

5 Read. Then write sentences.

> milk juice chocolate sandwich
> water salad ice cream

I like	It's good for me
I don't like	It's bad for me

1 milk, good *I like milk. It's good for me.* .

2 juice, good _____ .

3 chocolate, bad _____ .

4 sandwich, good _____ .

5 water, good _____ .

6 salad, good _____ .

7 ice cream, bad _____ .

6 What do these pets like? Match.

1 bird   **a** cheese

2 cat   **b** meat

3 dog   **c** milk

4 mouse   **d** bread

Are you hungry?

1 Look. Then complete.

1 _Are you_ thirsty?

Yes, I am.

2 _____ sad?

_____

3 _____ tired?

_____

4 _____ scared?

_____

2 Follow. Write the questions and answers.

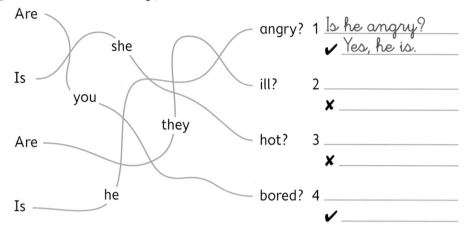

Are
she
Is
you
they
Are
he
Is

angry? 1 _Is he angry?_
✔ _Yes, he is._

ill? 2 _____
✗ _____

hot? 3 _____
✗ _____

bored? 4 _____
✔ _____

3 Use the words from the box and write. Then draw.

| hurt | happy | hot | hungry |

I'm _____ .

He's _____ .

She's _____ .

They're _____ .

8 I'm scared!

Read. Then match and draw.

1 There's a spider under my bed.

    a She's excited!

2 This is my brother. He likes chips.

    b I'm scared!

3 This is my Mum. It's her birthday today.

    c I'm happy!

4 I've got a beautiful puppy.

    d He's hungry!